WO

FREEDOM
IDEAS OF A NATION

Books in the series

B.R. Ambedkar

Aruna Asaf Ali

Maulana Abul Kalam Azad

Subhas Chandra Bose

Mohandas Karamchand Gandhi

Khan Abdul Ghaffar Khan

Sarojini Naidu

Jawaharlal Nehru

Vallabhbhai Patel

Rajendra Prasad

C. Rajagopalachari

Periyar E.V. Ramasami

Bhagat Singh

Rabindranath Tagore

WORDS OF FREEDOM
IDEAS OF A NATION

VALLABHBHAI PATEL

PENGUIN BOOKS

PENGUIN BOOKS

Published by the Penguin Group

Penguin Books India Pvt. Ltd, 11 Community Centre, Panchsheel Park, New Delhi 110 017, India

Penguin Group (USA) Inc., 375 Hudson Street, New York, New York 10014, USA

Penguin Group (Canada), 90 Eglinton Avenue East, Suite 700, Toronto, Ontario, M4P 2Y3, Canada (a division of Pearson Penguin Canada Inc.)

Penguin Books Ltd, 80 Strand, London WC2R 0RL, England

Penguin Ireland, 25 St Stephen's Green, Dublin 2, Ireland (a division of Penguin Books Ltd)

Penguin Group (Australia), 250 Camberwell Road, Camberwell, Victoria 3124, Australia (a division of Pearson Australia Group Pty Ltd)

Penguin Group (NZ), 67 Apollo Drive, Rosedale, North Shore 0632, New Zealand (a division of Pearson New Zealand Ltd)

Penguin Group (South Africa) (Pty) Ltd, 24 Sturdee Avenue, Rosebank, Johannesburg 2196, South Africa

Penguin Books Ltd, Registered Offices: 80 Strand, London WC2R 0RL, England

First published by Penguin Books India 2010

Anthology copyright © Penguin Books India 2010

All rights reserved

10 9 8 7 6 5 4 3 2 1

ISBN 9780143414018

Typeset in Perpetua by Eleven Arts, New Delhi

Printed at Thomson Press India Ltd, New Delhi

This book is sold subject to the condition that it shall not, by way of trade or otherwise, be lent, resold, hired out, or otherwise circulated without the publisher's prior written consent in any form of binding or cover other than that in which it is published and without a similar condition including this condition being imposed on the subsequent purchaser and without limiting the rights under copyright reserved above, no part of this publication may be reproduced, stored in or introduced into a retrieval system, or transmitted in any form or by any means (electronic, mechanical, photocopying, recording or otherwise), without the prior written permission of both the copyright owner and the above-mentioned publisher of this book.

Vallabhbhai Patel

It does not behove citizens of a free India. They have a duty and a right to tweak the two young men's ears and scold them. Only thus can things work out well.

I read in the papers that policemen are beaten up at some place or the other every day. Some time ago when the police opened fire somewhere, people clamoured for trials and inquiries. Why don't they make as much noise when policemen are beaten up? Has the Government to function or has it not? It can function well only if every free Indian realises that it is his duty to nurture and protect this freedom. The handful of people who are creating trouble should be curbed. Volunteer squads should be set up in localities where these things happen. There is talk of the underground. The son, the brother or the relation who works in the 'underground' should be warned to desist from the wrong path or be prepared to be turned over to the police. Without such active co-operation, things cannot be set right and the increasing expenditure finally falls on you. All the expenditure on police, jails, etc., comes from your pockets. It is diverted from the poor, needy refugees whom they are misleading. We may also have to provide for our brothers who are being persecuted in East Pakistan and for whom life has been made impossible.

If this thing goes on and they are hounded out, it will create a very difficult situation. So we should set our house in order. I beseech you to avoid internecine quarrels. Do not air your differences in such a way as to create a false impression among outsiders.

We have to advance productive work and increase the nation's wealth. We have to persuade the farmers to grow as much as they can, keep what they need for their own use and give the remainder to the Government at the appointed rates. There are those who incite the farmers to demand inflated rates. But where will the money come from? Not from those provocateurs but from you and me. We may have imposed controls and failed to check all graft and corruption, but we have not let anyone die of starvation, unlike what happened under the British in Bengal when thirty lakh people died. Crores of maunds of foodgrains have to be imported at great cost for this purpose.

Let us all sweat it out. Every Indian could share in the difficulties we face. If we share adversity for a year or two, we will have a happier prospect thereafter. Bengal must be restored to its rightful place in the forefront of Indian life.

To the Congress workers, my last appeal is to unite. All our lives, we have been devoting ourselves to suffering for the people. What does it matter if we get a ministry or not? You have fought famine and floods. Those who are not in the ministry find fault with it. This is no way to run the country. If some one does wrong, of course, he should be taken to task where it can be proved. Otherwise, we only spoil our own reputation. If the police show any shortcoming, the Government should be approached, but we must forget the old habit of criticising them in general terms. Today they work devotedly in difficult circumstances. We must give them our support and sympathy. To the newspapermen, the members of the professions and the intelligentsia, my appeal is that they should say and do what is right, raise their voices for the proper causes and raise volunteer squads to protect the honour of Calcutta and of Bengal.

Contents

Introduction — ix

1. Speech at the First Meeting of the Advisory Committee on Fundamental Rights — 1
2. First Tidings First — 7
3. Forget Your Mutual Quarrels — 21
4. The Mantle Will Now Fall on Young Shoulders — 29
5. The Right Atmosphere — 41
6. Build a Strong India — 47
7. In Years to Come — 69
8. Blueprint for Prosperity — 77
9. Disorder Hampers Progress — 93

Contents

Appendix

Three Years of Freedom　　　　113

Sources　　　　120

Introduction

Vallabhbhai Patel (31 October 1875–15 December 1950), fondly referred to as 'Sardar'—chief—and the 'Iron Man of India', was one of the foremost leaders of India's independence movement and is credited with the integration of the princely states into the Indian Union and the creation of the modern pan-Indian civil services.

A skilled and pragmatic politician, Vallabhbhai Patel was a man of both vision and action. His legendary organisational and administrative skills and his ability to clarify a situation and take decisive action set him apart from his contemporaries. A successful lawyer, Patel was inspired by Mahatma Gandhi's philosophy, and under Gandhi's tutelage began to take an active role in the freedom movement. Devoted to Gandhi, Patel adopted a simple lifestyle and abandoned the trappings of Western living. His involvement in the Borsad, Kheda and Bardoli satyagrahas, where farmers practised civil disobedience to protest against unjust British taxes, transformed him into one of the most powerful leaders in Gujarat and in the Indian National Congress.

Patel worked to organise the INC for elections in 1934 and 1937 and was one of the most vocal supporters of the Quit India movement. He was arrested and incarcerated time and again by the British for his principal role in the freedom struggle, notably when he was arrested for supporting Gandhi's salt satyagraha.

In the last years of the freedom struggle, the friction between Patel and Jawaharlal Nehru increased though Patel stepped aside in the elections for the presidency of the INC in 1946, at Gandhi's behest, to make way for Nehru. This ensured that Nehru, not Patel, would be the leader of the first government of Free India. Troubled by the friction

Introduction

between the two stalwarts of the INC, Gandhi counselled Patel to work with Nehru. As always, Patel complied and served as the first Home Minister and Deputy Prime Minister of India.

As Home Minister, Vallabhbhai Patel was charged with forging a united India from over 550 semi-autonomous princely states and colonial provinces, and was called upon to deal with the terrible circumstances in the aftermath of the partition. Patel's efforts provided safety and relief for refugees in Punjab and Delhi. He toured many regions marred by communal violence and exhorted the rioting masses to maintain law and order in his inimitable, quiet and sincere style. His legendary negotiation skills ensured almost all princely states acceded to India. States like Junagadh and Hyderabad that did not cooperate and struggled against joining the Indian Union were threatened with military action and Patel made good on the threat.

In his many speeches, he made a case for

Introduction

communal harmony; peace among different regions; the responsibility of common people in maintaining law and order; and his fervent belief that independence should not only be enjoyed by those who live in British-era provinces, but must be experienced by all the people of the country irrespective of their citizenship of one kingdom or the other. Marked by brevity, Patel's speeches outlined his unambiguous stance on issues. He was not given to elegant turns of phrase, nor was he an orator, but his speeches provide a glimpse of a realist who was able to reach out to millions and appeal to their best instincts. His efforts at creating a unified and united India where all the citizens enjoyed the fruits of the freedom struggle created the Indian Republic we know today.

SPEECH AT THE FIRST MEETING OF THE ADVISORY COMMITTEE ON FUNDAMENTAL RIGHTS

27 FEBRUARY 1947

GENTLEMEN, I THANK YOU MOST SINCERELY FOR THE HONOUR—THE GREAT HONOUR—THAT YOU HAVE CONFERRED UPON ME BY REPOSING YOUR CONFIDENCE IN ELECTING ME AS CHAIRMAN OF A COMMITTEE WHICH IS COMPOSED OF VARIOUS INTERESTS. This committee forms one of the most vital parts of the Constituent Assembly and one of the most difficult tasks that has to be done by us is the work of this committee. Often you must have heard in various debates in British parliament that have been held on this question recently and before when it has been claimed on behalf of the British Government that they have a special responsibility—a special obligation—for the protection of the interests of the minorities. They claim to have more special interest than we have. It is for us to prove that it is a bogus claim, a false claim and that nobody can be more interested than us in India in the protection of our minorities. Our mission is to satisfy every one of them and we hope we shall be able to satisfy every interest and safeguard the interest of all the minorities to their satisfaction. Let us hope that our deliberations will be so conducted that we can disillusion those who are looking with a critical eye from outside that we know how to conduct our business and we know how to rule better than those who claim that they can rule others. At least let us prove we have no ambition to rule others. In this committee, therefore, we begin our work today with a determination and a desire to come to decisions not by majority but by uniformity. Let us sink all our differences and look to one and one interest only, which is the interest of all of us—the interest of India as a whole.

FIRST TIDINGS FIRST

SPEECH AT
A PUBLIC MEETING
HELD IN CONNECTION
WITH THE INDEPENDENCE
WEEK CELEBRATIONS,

NEW DELHI, 11 AUGUST 1947

OUR FIRST TASK IS TO STABILISE, CONSOLIDATE AND STRENGTHEN OURSELVES AND THE REST CAN HAVE ONLY A SECONDARY PRIORITY. My colleagues and I have agreed to the partition of the country not because of fear or out of a sense of defeat. Under the prevailing conditions in the country partition on the present pattern was the best thing possible and I have no qualms about it. In a matter of weeks we have divided the country, the Army, the Services, etc., and this indeed has been a colossal task.

I, however, strongly believe that those who have seceded today will be disillusioned soon and their union with the rest of India is assured. What nature and God had intended to be one can on no account be split in two for all time.

I appeal to you to rub out from your minds the memories of the past two years, deem it as a terrible nightmare and forget it, and to look forward with single-minded purpose to make India strong, prosperous and happy. This can only be done by hard work. A Socialist Government in Britain is calling upon the workers to sweat an hour more a day and the strange contrast here is that our Socialists and others preach strikes and encourage wage-boosts. This can only result in printing more notes at Nasik and end up in serious trouble.

I welcome Mr Liaquat Ali Khan's latest statement and am happy that the minorities in Pakistan would be protected and their rights safeguarded. Such a generous move by the League cannot but evoke reciprocity here in India.

I am sure that all the Indian States will join the Indian Union and none can afford to keep out and live in isolation. First things should be done first and the first job is to get the States to accede to, and thereby consolidate, the Union. The demand of the people in the States for a democratic regime raises an entirely different issue. I cannot see how an Indian ruler can exist with his subjects in hostility and clamouring for popular Government.

The Congress was pledged to rid the country of foreign domination and after making considerable sacrifices and prolonged suffering it has succeeded. But the Congress has also worked for a united India and a union of all the communities and unfortunately it cannot claim any success there. This has been due to factors beyond our control. Our joy on 15 August would have been fuller and greater, had not India been divided; but this is not to be for the present.

I would make no efforts to explain away the responsibility of the Congress for dividing the country. We took these extreme steps after great deliberation. In spite of my previous strong opposition to partition, I agreed to it because I felt convinced that in order to keep India united it must be divided now.

My experience in office during the past year showed that it was impossible to do anything constructive with the Muslim League in. The League representatives during their continuance in office did nothing but create deadlocks and their role was entirely an obstructionist one. Besides, as I have already once said, I found that the Muslims (save for a few exceptions) engaged in all capacities in the Government were with the Muslim League. Thus the rot had set in and it could not be permitted to continue any longer except at the risk of a disaster for the whole country. Indeed at one stage—and it obtains even now to some degree—things had become so bad that, with the killing at Calcutta, riots spread all over and it became a perilous adventure for Hindus and Muslims to visit one another's localities. The economic life of the country was paralysed and there was little security of life or property.

The only way out of the sickening situation, the Congress realised, lay in the elimination of the third party, the British power. The British, on their part, declared that they would quit by June 1948. But the period was long. Also, their statement promising to hand over power to the authorities in the provinces gave rise to a vigorous effort to dislodge the Ministries in Assam, the Punjab and the Frontier. The League succeeded in the Punjab. Even though they failed in the Frontier and Assam, the League movement caused great misery and bloodshed.

In order to settle the issue immediately and prevent the slaughter of innocent people, the Congress decided to agree to the division of the country and demanded the partition of the Punjab and Bengal. This was no surrender to the League threats or policy of appeasement.

Today the partition of India is a settled fact and yet it is an unreal fact. The partition, I hope, however, removes the poison from the body politic of India. This, I am sure, would result in the seceding areas desiring to reunite with the rest of India.

India is one and indivisible. One cannot divide the set or split the running waters of a river. The Muslims have their roots in India. Their sacred places and their cultural centres are located here in India. I do not know what they can do in Pakistan and it will not be long before they begin to return.

Most of the opposition to the Congress in this partition came from quarters which had never in the past given evidence of any strength. Despite the division, it must be remembered, we have 80 per cent of the country with us which is a compact unit with great possibilities. Twenty per cent has gone over to Pakistan and I wish that State all success and prosperity.

I wish them to be strong because then

alone there can be friendly relations and amity between the two States. There can be no friendship between a strong unit and a weakling. India harbours no ill will towards Pakistan and will, in fact, do all in her power to help the new State.

The main task before India today is to consolidate herself into a well-knit and united power. The obstacle of foreign domination is now gone but there are serious problems that confront us. Economically India is in a sad plight. The war has resulted in making India a creditor nation but that does not mean much. The United Kingdom is our debtor and owes us a huge amount but she does not appear to have anything to pay us now. In fact the Big Powers have so arranged their economies that smaller and poorer countries remain at a disadvantage.

The Socialists in India are always talking of a Socialist Republic. Instead of restricting their activities to mere agitation, I would ask them to take over the administration of one province and solve the problems which have arisen in the wake of a prolonged war.

In contrast to their counterparts in Great Britain the Indian Socialists are pursuing an opposite course. Strikes are encouraged and higher wages demanded. If there is no water in the well, none can draw any to drink. By all means let them take away the wealth of a few rich in the country, but to what extent would this effort any relief to the poor— the teeming millions?

The need of the hour is to increase the wealth of the country and this can be done only by putting in more and more work and thus increasing production. This requires the maintenance of peace in the country. For one year now there has been disorder in the country. Now that Pakistan has been established, there is no quarrel between Hindus and Muslims. If, unfortunately, there should be a recurrence of this strife, it would not be the cowardly killings of innocent people but a battle between two armies of the two States.

I appeal to the people not to indulge in mutual strife but to create a calm atmosphere and engage themselves in constructive activities which are essential for the building up of a new India.

As regards the States question, the co-operation of all the rulers is necessary to consolidate and strengthen the Indian Union. When the foreign power has been eliminated, the Princes will have to adjust themselves to the new democratic order. The days of those rulers who do not command the confidence of their subjects are numbered. The majority of the States have acceded to the Union and I appeal to the rest to join the Union before 15 August. States which do not come in now but may decide to join at a later date would have to accede on different terms. These days no State can afford to live in isolation.

I ask the people to exercise reserve in judging the role of the Princes at the present juncture. The rulers have not been free up till now and many of them do not even now believe that Paramountcy is lapsing on 15 August. Many of them being descendants of great and benevolent rulers of the past ages, I have no doubt that they would not hesitate in pursuing a correct policy and becoming popular rulers.

Our problems are mainly domestic. Ever since I was released from prison, I have been saying that imperialism is on its last legs, not only in India but in all Asia. The British are quitting India and I think that Dutch imperialism will meet its end in Indonesia.

There cannot be in the future any more separate electorates or weightages and special treatment. Every community must get what is its due, but if a community which forms 15 per cent of the population has 60 per cent representation, say, in the Police Department, it undoubtedly creates a problem.

Vallabhbhai Patel

As regards the agitation for cow protection, I agree with the demand, but I ask why no such agitation was sponsored in the past. In countries where cows enjoy no legal protection, they are looked after much better and yield more milk. But at a time when the Government are faced with the problem of protecting human beings, the question of protecting cows cannot have priority. I deprecate attempts which are supposed to unite the country but in fact divide the Hindus. Nobody today, except the Congress, can undertake the task of uniting the country.

India has nothing but goodwill towards all, but if her safety is endangered she must have the strength to defend herself, and for this people must work.

FORGET YOUR MUTUAL QUARRELS

SPEECH AT PUBLIC MEETING,

PATIALA, 22 OCTOBER 1947

I RECALL HOW AFTER YEARS OF STRUGGLE AND SUFFERING INDIA HAS WON INDEPENDENCE AND SHAKEN OFF THE FOREIGN YOKE. All of us who took part in this struggle did so with the idea that when independence was achieved, there would be good Government in India. When we accepted partition, it was with the sincere desire that we should thereby be enabled to work out our own salvation, unhampered by the factors which rendered progress impossible. At the same time, we wished Pakistan well and hoped that under settled conditions, when they realised that we were really brothers and not two nations of different faiths and ideologies, they would come back to us. But the poison has been injected too far by the ceaseless propaganda of hate and of the two-nation theory.

The result has been that no Sikh and Hindu can live in peace and safety in Pakistan, a fact which had its reactions in that no Muslim could live without fear in East Punjab. Nevertheless, we have to so order our conduct that no further internecine quarrels taint our history. We must all live in amity and goodwill and must not tolerate 'Goonda Raj' which is being perpetrated in various areas owing to the spirit of lawlessness which the last few weeks have generated and promoted . . .

After alien rule, to which both the rulers of the States and the people were equally subjected has been removed, all those who are left belong to one family. There can, therefore, be no quarrel with the Princes.

They are ours and we can make them understand and appreciate our point of view. But, before you can make them understand

and ask them to relieve themselves of the burden which they are shouldering, it is your bounden duty to make yourselves worthy of taking over those responsibilities. It is not enough to ask for responsible Government. You must know how to digest it.

No Government can function without popular support. Travancore and Mysore are living examples of how in the fitness and fullness of time, popular unity and strength had made the rulers part with power. This shows that we must change our method to suit the new circumstances which the departure of alien rule has created.

I myself took part in many a fight with rulers in the past. But I always told them that my struggle was not with the rulers, but with those agents of alien power who were propping them up against popular demand and popular forces. But the days of vilifying Princes, calling them names and maligning them are gone. It is not only a waste of energy to concentrate on them, but also needless irritation and a profitless undertaking. Our methods now have to be guided by a more friendly approach and a spirit of understanding and goodwill. No Government anywhere in India can be carried on without popular support. I am sure the Princes themselves realise that their interests lie in taking the people with them. Why should we, therefore, pick quarrels or choose the path of ill will or hostility?

I appeal to you to cultivate a proper sense of moral values. I ask you do a little heart-searching. We can only advise you, but you can act on that advice only according to your capacity. If you are selfless workers, you will get your reward. But if you become involved in mutual jealousies and internecine quarrels, you can only do damage to the cause which you profess to uphold. When we achieved independence, it was with a view to carving out for India a place in the world polity, and to raising the stature and the standard of living of the people. Instead, we find ourselves fully preoccupied with the task of meeting the most gigantic problem of refugee relief that has ever faced man in human history.

This is not the time to involve ourselves in needless disputes, nor can we ever afford to follow the mirage of many 'stans' like Khalistans and Sikhistans or Jatistans. If we are not careful and become a prey to these inimical ideals, we can only succeed in turning India into a *pagalistan* (land of lunatics). It is, therefore, up to you to forget your mutual quarrels and behave with a sense of responsibility and in a spirit of co-operation and goodwill. We have formidable tasks before us. Attacks on railways, looting and the part which sometimes even the military and the police play in such incidents merely show that we are face to face with moral bankruptcy, which, if not checked, must mean downfall and ruin.

Remember, if a hungry man dies of starvation, he dies without a stain on his honour. But one who steals to feed himself virtually suffers from living death. He has not followed the path of honour and glory, but that of shame and disgrace. If we want popular Government, we must build up popular support and strength. Princes want respect and reverence. They will gracefully yield to popular demands if they find that a sense of responsibility and popular support prompts the popular organizations. I, therefore, ask such organizations to work selflessly and in a spirit of public service and thereby earn, not only the gratitude of the people but also the confidence of the rulers and achieve the object which is neither inimical to the interests of the Princes nor inconsistent with their responsibilities. For, after all, no Prince can afford to treat popular support with contempt, nor popular grievances with indifference.

THE MANTLE WILL NOW FALL ON YOUNG SHOULDERS

JAIPUR, 17 DECEMBER 1947

THERE ARE ABOUT 500 SMALL INDIAN PRINCELY STATES—MORE THAN THE TOTAL NUMBER OF INDEPENDENT STATES IN THE WORLD. The former alien rulers of India preserved them like pickles, but now Paramountcy has gone, foreign rule has gone and India has become free. But we have not yet breathed the real air of freedom. So many people do not know that we have got Swaraj, though they know that foreign rule is gone. People do not yet have any taste of it. They do not know whether we have gained anything from it. We must make them realise the difference between foreign rule and Swaraj.

It is true we have not yet had time. During the short time that has elapsed, we have had, due to our misfortune, communal troubles. The poison of hatred generated by the League gripped us. We accepted even partition of India in the hope that it would restore peaceful conditions. That was not to be. If we had not been hit by this cataclysm, we would have been much better off. Fortunately, Jaipur has escaped and I congratulate its people and Government on it. The model which you have placed before the world is one which your people can be proud of, but what about the future? We will not stand still, we have to march forward. I am confident that it will not be necessary for me or you to ask for responsible Government from the Jaipur Maharaja. Whatever you want you are sure to get. The Maharaja of Jaipur and his advisers have worked together with us in unifying India. I know they are with us and have shared with us in the achievement of freedom.

In every State people demand responsible

Government. The rulers are aware of this and know that they have to march with the times. At the same time we should be clear about our own duty. It is our right to take over Government from them, but if we cannot improve upon it and provide better administration, what is the advantage?

The Congress has not demanded power for the sake of power but for the sake of service. If you have narrow ideas like Sikhistan, Jatistan and Rajasthan, I should like to say that the world today is different. We cannot think of any such narrow ideology. Government must be that of the people—rich, poor, Hindu, Muslim, Parsee and Christian.

We have to conduct Governmental affairs in a manner that each one feels it is his own Government. Times are such that Government is of those who exert and not of those who sit idle. You should be certain how and for what purpose you use power. We have to utilise power for the welfare of the downtrodden.

I find in the State there are the Praja Mandal and Congress, Hindu Sabha, R.S.S., Rajput Sabha, Jat Sabha and so on. This will not do. You have yet to get together and work together.

You have expressed the hope that Hyderabad shall also join the Indian Union within one year. I have no doubt that it will. It will realise that its interests demand it. The people demand self-government in Hyderabad. They have a right to do so. How can Hyderabad remain isolated? It will come of its own accord.

Muslims demand parity when Hindus are 85 per cent and Muslims 15 per cent. Responsible men should not talk like this. Some say they have connections with Pakistan. If that is so, they will have to bear the consequences.

Kashmir is a different problem. The Pakistan Government is saying that the tribesmen have become infuriated and are attacking, looting, etc. But everyone knows it is not the work merely of raiders. There can be no doubt that there are some regular troops armed with automatic weapons. It is our duty to stand by Kashmir and we will discharge that duty. India will not desert Kashmir even if the struggle goes on for ten years. But ultimately it will be for the people of Kashmir to decide their own fate, and this can be possible only when the last raider has left the State. There is, therefore, no cause for worry, but the people of Jaipur can assist the Government of India by spreading the message that there should be no trouble elsewhere.

I have received complaints against the Rashtriya Swayamsevak Sangh. If so many complaints are received, the Sangh should realise that there must be something wrong. I appreciate the enthusiasm of young men, but that should be diverted into constructive channels.

There is a great deal to be done to make India militarily strong. Very substantial industrial effort must back the army. All that cannot be achieved by the lathis of the Sangh which are being used for breaking the heads of a handful of Muslims. There is no point in your hoping to get Pakistan back into the Indian Union. It will come of its own accord and we should, therefore, let the Pakistanis remain as they are. I am certain that whether they grow strong or weak, ultimately it would be better for us to get them back when they themselves feel like doing so.

A strong army requires strong support in the matter of supply and food. The people have, therefore, to husband their resources and for that purpose they must forget their quarrels.

We old men have completed our mission. India has secured her freedom. The mantle will now fall on young shoulders and they should be ready to undertake it. They cannot do this if they waste their efforts over trifles. If they follow the path, which the Sangh has been following, they would be doing a disservice to the country.

Everyone realises that in order to subsist

as a great nation India must produce more, but instead of that, agitators are compelling workers to strike, the latest instance being in Calcutta where the popular Government wants special powers but obstruction is placed in its way. Firing had to be resorted to, but the reply is a threat of a general strike to compel the withdrawal of the Bill.

There is no question now of foreigners being given special powers. It is a representative Government which can be changed if people want it to be changed. Let those who feel that urge to advise a general strike ponder over the reception which was accorded to our leader, Pandit Nehru, when he went to Calcutta. He was greeted by a million people.

It is only agitators who clamour for strikes. India is not going to benefit by these tactics. We cannot afford to waste a single hour. It is essential for our existence that we should produce. If we still do not realise this, we are doomed.

Land has been concentrated in the hands of a minority of people in States like Jaipur. I appeal to landholders not to live on the earnings of those who shed their sweat and blood to make the soil productive. It does not behove Rajputs whose duty it is to protect others to live at the expense of others. Let them make sacrifices so that others may live.

It was by disunity that India lost its freedom. Hundreds of years ago, despite the feats of valour and heroism performed by men and women in Rajputana, India became a slave to foreigners. The people should not repeat those mistakes now.

In the address, I have also been asked to say something about Junagadh, but there is hardly anything to be said. The people of Junagadh will deal with the problem. The problem of the States now consists of Hyderabad and Kashmir. I have every hope Hyderabad will do the right thing before the year is out. In this world the popular will can be ignored only at one's peril.

Vallabhbhai Patel

When such a big power as the British had to quit India under the pressure of popular opinion, how can the Nizam hope to do otherwise? However, the new Government which has just assumed office should be given a chance. Some people fear that in the interim period Hyderabad will be prepared for a struggle. Even if that is true, it is foolish to imagine that we would sit idle while these preparations are being made.

I appeal to you to follow implicitly the constructive programme laid down by Mahatma Gandhi.

THE RIGHT ATMOSPHERE

SPEECH TO A GATHERING OF VILLAGERS WHILE OPENING A LIBRARY AT MEHRAULI,

DELHI, 29 DECEMBER 1947

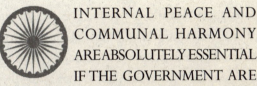 INTERNAL PEACE AND COMMUNAL HARMONY ARE ABSOLUTELY ESSENTIAL IF THE GOVERNMENT ARE TO GO AHEAD WITH THEIR PLANS FOR IMPROVING THE LOT OF THE COMMON MAN IN INDIA. Disturbed conditions are detrimental to your own interests. Leave the work of fighting to the Government and we shall fight the real enemy of India.

We have fought against foreign domination because we wanted to drive away poverty from our country and make the life of its people worth living. What is the good of our achieving independence if Indians continue to be poor and if no difference is felt with the coming in of the National Government?

The real work has not been completed. Actually it was to start now. But the time since 15 August, short but precious, has been lost in communal fighting thus nothing constructive could be done. The President of the local Congress Committee has drawn my attention to the poverty prevailing among the people of Mehrauli, but if they want the Government to do something about it, they must first create the right atmosphere. They must have a clean slate before any step could be taken.

A large number of Muslims had been living in Mehrauli but now they have left the place. The same kind of thing has happened in Delhi, the capital of India, and that is really deplorable. The communal rioting has given India a bad name abroad and provided the foreigners with a chance to say that the Indians are not capable of managing their own house.

All hopes of bringing about a radical

change in the living conditions of the people of India have come to naught, because the entire resources of the Government are employed in maintaining law and order. You must cooperate with us, and all that we ask of you is to keep peace. These disturbances have been a terrible strain on the finances of the country. You must realise that nearly Rs 4 lakh are being spent every day on the Kashmir operations alone. We shall continue work in Kashmir and shall not concede even an inch of our country. The people must face the fact that Pakistan has been established and that those Muslims who wanted to migrate to it have done so already. Those who elected to remain in India could with no justification be asked to leave the country. I appeal to you to create such an atmosphere that no Muslim may feel unsafe among you.

If you are attacked, fight back by all means, but no one should commit such acts of barbarity as killing innocent women, children and patients in hospitals.

BUILD A STRONG INDIA

SPEECH AT ISLAND GROUNDS,
MADRAS, 23 FEBRUARY 1949

YOU WANT ME TO TALK TO YOU IN ENGLISH. I shall obey your command; but take it from me that it will not be long before you yourselves will have to speak in our national language. If you do not do that, you will drag the country backward. We have to exert our maximum effort to go forward. Unless you do that, I am afraid, you will suffer.

After a prolonged struggle the country has secured freedom, but it is not freedom of the kind that we wanted. It is not freedom of the kind that the deliverer of the country expected, and to our shame we have to confess that by our folly we have lost him. Now after his going we must do penance and try our best to deserve the freedom that he obtained for us.

Free India is only a child of a year and a half. It has yet to learn to walk; it has to grow, to be strong, and its future depends upon how we build today. Therefore, we have to nurse it carefully; we have to feed, clothe and strengthen it properly. It is our great good fortune that we have here a rare opportunity to build our own country in our own fashion. History will record what we are doing today.

The first requisite for building a strong, free India is unity and peace. If there is no unity in the country, it is bound to go down. Therefore, we must first of all adjust our differences and behave in such a manner that there is complete harmony and peace in the country. You cannot expect the Government continuously to maintain peace by force. It would be an evil day when in this country the Government has to use repressive measures permanently. Today we are passing through a period of crisis and our young men have, in their impatience, not realised that the freedom which has been obtained with great difficulty is likely to be lost or likely to give no benefit, no advantage, if we do not appreciate that our present duty is to unite and consolidate our freedom.

We lost our leader because we forgot the very first lesson. If we do not realise even after his going that in unity lies our strength, then greater misfortune will befall us.

For unity, we must forget differences of caste and creed and remember that we are all Indians, and all equal. There can be no distinction between man and man in a free country. All must have equal opportunities, equal rights and equal responsibilities. This is difficult for achievement in practice, but we must continuously strive towards that end.

There is one other thing that we have to do to maintain peace and order in this country. For a few years at least, till we are able to stand on our own legs, we must forget that we can every now and then threaten the Government. We cannot function if the Government is to be challenged day after day by groups of people who want to have their own way. What they want may be, according to their own honest thinking, very good; but Gandhiji has put before us the ideal of obtaining what we want by peaceful methods and through truth and non-violence. If people begin to threaten and challenge Government's authority and try to overthrow it to gain their objectives by force, the latter would not be able to do anything constructive. Forces are existing in this country which would create chaos and disorder, which would weaken the country instead of strengthening it.

We in the Government have been dealing with the R.S.S. movement. They want that Hindu Rajya or Hindu culture should be imposed by force. No Government can tolerate this. There are almost as many Muslims in this country as in the part that has been partitioned away. We are not going to drive them away. It would be an evil day if we started that game, in spite of partition and whatever happens. We must understand that they are going to stay here and it is our obligation and our responsibility to make them feel that this is their country. It is, of course, their responsibility, on the other hand, to discharge their duties as citizens of this country.

We must all understand that partition is behind us. It has to come to stay. I honestly believe that it is good for both the new nations to be rid of a perpetual source of trouble and quarrels. In two hundred years of slavery, the administration created a situation in which we began to drift away from each other. It is good that we have agreed to partition in spite of all its evils; I have never repented my agreeing to partition. From the experience of one year of joint administration when we have not agreed to partition, I know we would have erred grievously and repented if we had not agreed. It would have resulted in a partition not into two countries but into several bits. Therefore, whatever some people may say, I am convinced and I remain convinced that our having agreed to partition has been for the good of the country.

After partition, we had a huge problem; those who partitioned the country with our concurrence had mental reservations; they thought that partition into two is not the last word and they started their game immediately after partition. They went to Junagadh in the midst of the Kathiawar States, where nearly half the number of princely states are located. From the middle of that group, they took Junagadh and secured its accession to Pakistan. It was the first danger sign, the signal for dividing India again. Fortunately for us, we woke up in time and those who tried that game saw that we are not sleeping. Simultaneously, there was trouble in Kashmir. Although there were many difficulties, the Government of India, despite all the impediments, got the situation under control rapidly. I should say we enhanced our reputation by sending there our army, which, in spite of its complete Indianisation, has proved its mettle and proved its worth. It is a great thing that immediately after the partition of the army and the partition of the country, our army, manned absolutely by our own people, showed by their strategy, their valour and their organising ability that it can stand comparison with any army in the world. It is a great gain.

Then our neighbour gave us long sleepless nights. Often, people were angry with us and thought we were neglecting the South. They hardly knew our difficulties and our plans. These plans cannot be revealed. What would happen if Hyderabad was invaded from the outside or if Hyderabad attacked us. We had to make preparations all over India. You know now by the results that we have kept our promise to perform the operation in such a manner that there is the least possible bleeding. This is what we have to show for the first year of our freedom.

People are impatient; they want more wages for labour. Do they think we want to starve labour? Are we foreigners? Some people say we are capitalist agents. One thing I learnt from Mahatma Gandhi is that a public man should not have any property, and can challenge any Government or any Communist to play this game with me. But my quarrel is what those who, contrary to the second part of Mahatmaji's advice to us, want to use violence. There should be no terrorism amongst ourselves. So long as people were playing that game when we were under a foreign power, we made allowance for it; we are paying for it also, because an evil once tolerated grows. That is what we see in Hyderabad.

Why are these Communists creating trouble there? How did they grow? It was because the Hyderabad Government was foolish enough to allow them to grow for its own ends and we had no control over them then to be able to suppress them. And what is it that we see there now? In three or four months' time, 200 or more young Congressmen, their own brothers, have been murdered. Is it a sign of freedom that in the first year of freedom you have 200 Congressmen killed in cold blood in a small area? Once these terrorists are driven out from that area, where will they go? Inside your border. They will harass you; they will play the same game with you. To the Communists, my appeal may be in vain, because they do not listen. I told them immediately after my release from jail last time that I was prepared to take all the Communists into the Congress, to forget the past and keep the doors open provided they give up violence and cease to draw their inspiration from foreign countries. Even now our offer is open, but if terrorism is the only method they want to employ, because they cannot defeat us at the polls and separate us from the masses of India, then it is our misfortune that we have to put our own dear young men and women into prison or to drive them underground.

That is one section of the people, with whom we have to deal; the other is the R.S.S. I have made them an open offer: 'Change your plans, give up secrecy, eschew communal conflict, respect the Constitution of India, show your loyalty to the Flag and make us believe that we can trust your words. To say one thing and to do another is a game which will not do.' In one year of freedom we have experienced many things and learnt many lessons. Whether they are friends or foes, whether they are our own dear young children, we are not going to allow them to play with fire, so that the house is not set on fire. It would be criminal to allow young men to indulge in acts of violence and destruction, to let the lessons that our neighbouring countries have learnt be wasted on us.

Thus I have spoken to the R.S.S. and to

the Communists. Then you have our Sikh friends. Some of them have also begun to threaten us and throw challenges. They are the only community in India which is allowed, with the unanimous voice of the Constituent Assembly, to keep arms. No other community is allowed to keep a sword or a kirpan. Why did we do this? Not in order that they might threaten the Government with the use of force. Government is prepared to hand over power to anybody who can take the people with him. But if anybody is going to play false and threaten the popular Government, the latter will not fail the people.

These are some of the many forces we are handling simultaneously in the first or second year of our freedom. We know that we have your affection, your love, your confidence, but that is not enough. You have seen our friends in the railways threaten us. They say there is going to be a strike in the railways if we do not meet their demands.

We are willing to do so if we can. We would be most anxious to do so. But I must point out to those who are in charge of the railway union that there are millions in this country who do not get as much as the railwaymen get: let them not create forces which they will not be able to control; let the railwaymen understand that it is also their duty to share the misfortunes of the people in a period of trouble. Let us tide over the difficulty first. After all, the railway is a nationalised concern; it is not a private company. Imagine the consequences, in this period of trouble, if railwaymen do not play their part. If there is a strike on the railways and we have to move the army from one place to another with railway communications cut off, what will happen? We continuously need to move food from one place to another swiftly, as we are faced with the threatened famine. If during such a period the South Indian Railway, which has threatened to strike, goes on strike, who will starve, and what would be the consequences? When the Railway Federation suspended its strike threat and kept it in abeyance, the other group called them capitalist agents. Now these other people have called for a strike; they know that they are in a minority and they will not succeed in making the railwaymen go on strike. So their only weapon is terrorism, sabotage, dislocation and disorder.

The Provincial Governments naturally have to tackle these people and immediately the Federation comes in with a statement that it is a wrong policy. I would like to know what is the right policy. When a house is on fire, is it the right policy to throw petrol or kerosene on it, or water?

We are living in very difficult times; yet the heart of the country is sound. The whole country knows that we are carrying an unbearable burden. Yet if anyone wants to see what the country thinks, let him come to the polls; I am prepared to accept the challenge. I am prepared to vacate as many seats as you like and have a trial of strength. And if you are able to take the country with you, we shall bless you, because the country is not going to follow any path which is foreign to Indian culture and civilisation and the path that Mahatma Gandhi has shown. But I want to ask you, why a few people round about the border of Hyderabad are terrorising the people in Krishna district? It is the fault of Congressmen. Are they united? Why are they quarrelling? Why do they not understand their responsibility? We made all kinds of sacrifices all our lives. Why did we make these sacrifices? Let not South India lose its good name and reputation. I appeal to you to realise what is happening. Did you ever imagine that Gandhiji would hear of a Congressman murdering a Congressman, or a Congressman instigating or helping a Communist to murder another Congressman? If the South Indian Railway is threatened, or if those railwaymen who work in South India are asked to go on strike, have you no responsibility? Everyone in India has to realise that, as a free citizen of India, he must shoulder graver and greater responsibility, if India is to take its proper place amongst the nations of the world.

Yesterday, I was presented an address by the Chambers of Commerce. It was in fact a catalogue of grievances. I had to tell them the unpleasant truth that unless everybody in this country, that is businessmen, labourers, industrialists, students and Government, all combine and co-operate, we are not going to make progress. We have not yet put democracy on a sound basis. In a democracy, of course, it is the will of the people that prevails, but the people must have experience to make their own free will felt and must have the responsibility to see that everyone is going to fulfil his obligations.

In this country, the greatest need of the hour is food. We import millions of tons of food into our country. We have not got the ships to bring the food that we want. So we pay crores of rupees as freight charges simply to bring the food here. We have not enough boats even to catch fish. We have no mercantile marine. We have nothing left in this country; for the last 200 years it has been bled white; during the war years in particular, every ounce of blood has been taken out. Our railway system has been completely disorganised. The Transport Member makes tremendous efforts to set it right. But the railways are like a decrepit old widow. Railway sleepers and rails were taken out and sent to various theatres of war. We cannot replace the wagons which have been overused for so many years. We cannot get locomotives. We cannot make them here; we have yet to establish factories for meeting the requirements of our country.

We must have a good mercantile marine; so we are building a fine port at Visakhapatnam. But it is only a beginning. A small country like Portugal has got pockets on our soil; we also have French colonies. Our friends in these areas who are fighting for freedom along with us ask us to first settle this question; others talk of the wages for labour; and still others want us to deal with the businessmen first and to give them their due. The businessmen are frightened of the talk of nationalisation. They say: 'Unless you give us conditions in which industry can thrive, we cannot invest money or we cannot get money. So production has been at a standstill. We cannot produce more wealth in this country.' The Communists and the Socialists say: 'let us first divide whatever is left and be all poor.' But if you do not produce anything, then neither you, nor any other section of the people will have anything. Therefore, so far as food is concerned, I have a grievance against Congressmen and against those people who were in the Congress and today are preaching to peasants not to help this Government in procurement and to ask for more money. They are no better than the other people who say: 'Do not work, stop work, go slow, ask for more wages.' Because if there is no procurement, then the only course open to us is to import more and more, and importing more is nothing but economic ruin of this country.

If we in this country realise our responsibility, there will be no dearth of food. Of course, there is scarcity to a certain extent; the shortage of food according to our statistics is 7 per cent. In a vast country like this, if we act up to our responsibilities, this is negligible. Many people waste their food and cook more than they should. Those people should put a stop to this wastage. Then we should produce more food. Every inch of land that is available should be used for growing vegetables, fruits and other food. Wherever there is waste land which can be reclaimed, it would be the duty of Government, local bodies, zamindars, and every citizen of India to use all his resources in the immediate task of growing more food on it. Thirdly, whatever surplus you have got, give it to the Government. When your neighbours are starving, do not be selfish. That is not the way which Gandhiji showed us. That is not our culture. Let not our neighbour starve; we must share his misery. Educate the peasants; tell them it is a religious duty to give all their surplus for Government procurement, so that Government can decrease the imports that are being made.

There are many Congressmen who are indifferent to this matter. They think that elections are coming and they will be unpopular if they ask for procurement. A greater crime is committed by those who teach the peasants to ask for higher prices and not to give crops for procurement. That is a crime against humanity. A real Congressman would say: 'My friends, our neighbours are dying; our country is being ruined; let us share the suffering of our brothers.' I am saying hard things to Congressmen because they have a greater responsibility, greater influence and a greater hold on the people.

Let us all put our heads as well as our hands together, tighten up our belts and be prepared to share the sufferings for a while. It is only for a while, because I assure you that the economy of the country is sound; the heart of the country is sound; there is immense wealth in the country. The country is full of mineral resources and wealth. We have simply to use our brains and our resources to take them out and use them. But it will take time; it is not an easy thing. We shall require experts, machinery and capital goods. If we tide over this short period, India will be flowing with milk and honey.

I am extremely touched by the affection that you have shown me. I have said some things which may be harsh, but however bitter they may be, they are a dose of medicine. In return for your affection, I can only ask you to forgive me if I have said anything harsh; take it as a piece of advice which comes from an honest and humble servant.

IN YEARS TO COME

SPEECH AT A RECEPTION HELD ON HIS SEVENTY-FIFTH BIRTHDAY,

DELHI, 31 OCTOBER 1949

I AM OVERWHELMED BY THE AFFECTIONATE WELCOME EXTENDED TO ME. Your good wishes and blessings are an inspiration to me to live and serve. It has been a difficult year for me. For mere bodily troubles, however, I do not care. Dust returns to dust. But the fact that this has been a very difficult year for the country worries me day and night. The coming year may be even more critical. One wrong step can bring the country to ruin.

My seventy-four years are a fairly long life span in a country like India. There is not much time left to me in this world. But what departure could be better than to depart with all the love that you have shown. I can only pray to God to make me every day more deserving of your blessings as long as I live. But India's leader, our helmsman, is abroad these days. Mine is a limited role—to strengthen his hands as long as I can. He is exerting himself to enchance the honour of our country. Of course it was Gandhiji above all who gained for India a place of honour in the world by the way he lived and still more by the way he died. Next to him, our leader has raised the status of our country by the spirit with which he is doing his work abroad. For true honour, however, and for the protection for our integrity, we should set our house in order. Honour abroad without strength at home cannot last long. We have to live up to the expectations we raise in the world.

People, both from within and outside the Congress, are criticising us. Some go to the extent of saying that British rule was better. This is unfortunate because when we think like this, we show a preference for slavery. But we should not forget that our centuries old slavery was a burden set so oppressively on our chest, that we could not even breathe. We have thrown off that burden but have yet to recover our breath. New life is being infused into an almost dead body. We are not yet fit to walk. If we try to run before we have learnt how to walk, we will break our legs.

Let no one think that we are ignorant of hunger and want in the country. If we were so ignorant, Mr Churchill would have been right in saying that the Government of this country had been handed over to 'men of straw'. But even he realises now that these are not then 'men of straw' but men of a peculiar strength. It should not be forgotten that there is suffering everywhere in the world. What we need is economic independence and that is not easy of attainment. There are so many barriers to be crossed. Devaluation has also created many difficulties which the peasant in the field and the labourer in the factory cannot realise. But those who fear difficulties can achieve nothing. Whatever the difficulties, there is a power in man which can face them and overcome them. But it is given to man, not cowards, to achieve this.

You must understand that great sacrifices will be needed to achieve economic independence, sacrifices of a nature different from those made in the freedom struggle; and all classes will have to contribute, the farmers, the factory workers, the rich as well as the middle-class people who are already hard pressed. The hardship may be less in the case of the rich, even none, let us presume. But in our country rich persons are very few. Ours is a poor country with a sprinkling of the rich. It is no use chasing them all the time. I will deal with them any way you like, but I know we have few men of experience in our country today.

It is the bulk of the people who must tighten their belts. Do not give to the

Government if you cannot afford it. Deposit what you can as a loan. Not only will our future be ensured but industry also will get a boost. Today we do not have enough financial resources for expanding industry and producing wealth. But if each individual makes his contribution in the form of savings, the savings of crores of people will go a long way towards achieving economic independence. There is no other way. From those who are wealthy we will try to get by persuasion. They will not be left out. But you must not say that we should take from them first and you will only follow later. There should be some kind of healthy competition here.

I have no fear of internal dangers now. Whenever there is danger from outside, the world will share the risk, because the Big Powers, affluent though they are, are always afraid lest another country became more powerful. Gandhiji taught us to shun fear. People of diverse faiths should live together and not quarrel among themselves. It is one thing if some Big Powers clash, but small powers cannot cast an evil eye on us. If they do, they will perish. We do not want to attack or coerce or plunder any country. But we want to make our country strong. In this you should all cooperate. If in this work I have your blessings, my life would be more worth living.

BLUEPRINT FOR PROSPERITY

BROADCAST ON
THE BIRTH ANNIVERSARY
OF JAWAHARLAL NEHRU,

14 NOVEMBER 1949

I AM VERY GLAD TO BE BROADCASTING TODAY, THE BIRTHDAY OF MY DEAR BROTHER JAWAHARLAL. The day is twice blessed; not only are we celebrating a great national event, but we are also welcoming him back with all our heart after an eventful tour abroad.

Our birthday gift to him is loyalty and devotion; he has returned it with compound interest by raising our country's status abroad, and by presenting a sum total of goodwill and friendship which he has engendered wherever he has gone during his tour. He returns today again to resume the heavy burden of responsibilities which attach to his high office. Let us offer him our felicitations as well as our prayers.

How heavy that burden is and how great those responsibilities, you must have guessed in some measure from the speech I delivered on Saturday, 11 November 1949, about our economic situation. I wish once again to emphasise the gravity of the situation that faces us and of the immensity of the task that lies ahead, if we are to stage a quick and permanent recovery. I can tell you quite frankly that the time for preparing paper schemes has gone; we cannot indulge any longer in the pastime of conjuring before our vision idealistic Utopias. We have to live among the hard facts of today, and it is in that realistic atmosphere that we have to think and act. It is no use our offering to a hungry man a rich fare some time hence. I have been constantly laying stress on the need for self-sufficiency in food and cloth, our basic wants. We have spent crores on our food production drive without making any appreciable difference to our heavy imports, the crushing burden of which is visible in our dwindling foreign currencies and balances.

We have in hand so many schemes of irrigation. We have a huge area of cultivable waste which is waiting for the hands that can plough. Even the areas under cultivation can, with diligence and well-directed efforts, be made to yield more. We have a big reclamation programme which is being financed from the money that we have borrowed from abroad. In addition, we have programmes in India for subsidising schemes of food production. If we can concentrate on all these, I have no doubt that, in spite of the economic situation of today, we can produce enough to feed ourselves and reduce the heavy drain of freight and profits which we obligingly remit to foreign growers and shippers.

Just think of it. If we had at our disposal the amount which we have spent on food imports during the last three years, we could have completely rehabilitated those unfortunate brothers and sisters of our who have had to leave their hearths and homes in Pakistan and who are still looking up to us for relief and succour. My heart bleeds to see so many of my unfortunate countrymen living in conditions of filth and poverty. Let those who pass by them reflect for a moment how they themselves are contributing to their misery by failing in their duty to help themselves and help us in ensuring self-sufficiency in food.

We always speak of India's culture, of India's civilisation, but do we ever pause to think that the relief of the poor, mutual aid amongst neighbours, charity to the helpless and kindness to the downtrodden have been the shining virtues of that culture and civilisation? Let us ask ourselves if we are living in the spirit of those ancient virtues. We are honest, we shall point the finger of scorn at all of us who demand their pound of flesh for every seer of scorn that they hand over to Government, or who store up their corn even though they see their next-door neighbour starving. The same applies to those who do not work assiduously to produce more from every inch of their soil, or who not only allow land to go waste but also allow foodgrains to deteriorate.

Are we to take Gandhiji's name only when it suits our purpose? I should like to ask all those who swear by him how they reconcile their professions of faith in his mission with the everyday breach of the principles which he taught.

My appeal to the agriculturists is to work and work hard with a will to get the best out of their exertion and deliver to Government the maximum they can spare on the basis of their minimum requirements. They should help Government to implement the many programmes of increasing food production so that we can restore the balance between supply and demand of foodgrains as quickly as possible. Whatever area can be brought under cultivation must be utilised to produce foodgrains.

My next appeal is to the industrialists, businessmen, traders and labour. I need not stress here the importance which increasing production has in our plants to deal with the present economic crisis. In many ways it is our one and only hope to correct the maladjustment between supply and demand and thereby reverse the rising spiral of prices. Government, industry and labour must all play the game in a spirit of national service. We must all have the fullest sense of a national emergency; we must close our ranks as we do in the presence of a common danger; we must tighten our belts to give the nation the tribute we owe to it; we must all contribute our mite to the creation of that huge reservoir of funds both here and abroad, which we need to back our national effort for a happier and better state of living.

Let industrialists concentrate on getting the maximum out of their plants and machinery; let labour lend their helping hand to the industrialists to exploit their resources to the maximum national advantage. It will be Government's duty to ensure that the decks are cleared for action and there are no impediments, no bottle-necks and no red tape. The wheels must move with clock-wise precision and perfect smoothness and there must be no mutual fault-finding. The tradesmen have also to do their part. It is their duty to ensure that the produced articles reach the consumer with the minimum of difficulty and minimum of extra cost. None wishes to deprive them of their due but it would be a national crime for anyone to take more than one's due. On the other hand, even if one has to sacrifice something of his due for the sake of delivering the goods to the nation, that must be cheerfully faced. In such an inexorable and unrelenting struggle for existence, mercenary motives must not be allowed to rule to the exclusion of patriotic duty.

Let me also make a special appeal to

those who have money to spare. It is, I know, a large body of heterogeneous elements. We are not spendthrifts as a nation; saving is our national instinct, whether we are agriculturists, labourers, businessmen, lawyers, civil servants or traders. They must all save every pie they can and place their savings at the disposal of Government for utilisation in national-building enterprises. We had a plethora of development schemes in the hope of large balances being available for expenditure. Now when we took stock of our position, we found that if we were to live within our means, we had drastically to cut our development programme.

It is obvious that we cannot keep this programme in suspense for very long without doing grave damage to our national economy. These programmes are our only hope if we have to feed not only the present, but the increasing population of our country. They afford the only chance of increased industrialisation, without which it will not be possible for us either to maintain or to improve upon our present standard of living. We must, therefore, restore our economy to a position in which we can implement these programmes to the best of our capacity and in an efficient and businesslike manner. For all this, we must have capital, and that capital must come from our own country. We may be able to borrow from international markets here and there, but obviously we cannot base our everyday economy on foreign borrowing.

In my speech on Saturday I have already indicated why and how the investor should place confidence in us. I stated that a point had been reached when nobody who can save or has saved can afford to withhold investing it in a profitable undertaking without incurring the odium of having failed the country in its hour of crisis. Indeed, it would be as wrong for anyone not to invest savings as it would be in times of war for anyone to shirk the obligation of compulsory national service. This brings me to commend to you the scheme, which we have announced, of voluntary cuts in higher salaries and compulsory savings, for Government servants have in this matter given a lead to business and professions which the latter would do well to follow. I am separately making an appeal to Provincial Governments to evolve similar schemes for their own employees. We hope shortly to supplement our own scheme by a similar scheme for Government servants drawing Rs 250 and below. When that scheme is announced, I am sure Provinces will follow suit.

I would now appeal to business-houses, commercial establishments and men engaged in different professions and other institutions employing any substantial staff to adapt our scheme to the conditions of their own organisation and to implement it cheerfully and in a spirit of self-sacrifice for the country's needs.

All these contributions would, while

assuring to the contributors some saving for future needs, assist Government considerably in strengthening its ways and means position and would enable it to finance the many schemes of development which on account of the necessity for imposing rigid economy have had to be suspended or drastically curtailed. 'Spend less, save more, and invest as much as possible' should henceforward be the motto of every citizen in the country and all of you must see that it becomes the guiding principle of your life. You can select for yourself any suitable means of investment which are open to you, but only make sure that all the money that you save is spent for a national cause.

I shall now say a word to those Government servants to whom has fallen and will continue to fall, the implementation of the many measures of control and of regimentation of everyday affairs of the citizen which we have to enforce. It is a great responsibility. The powers which wield, if rightly used, can bring the nation heavy dividends, but the same, if abused, can bring not only harm but disrepute. They have the reputation of many citizens in their hands. They will very often find that a kind word, a sympathetic gesture and an attitude of understanding coupled with honesty and integrity will enable them to do their work much quicker and much better than snobbery, a sense of superiority and such other departures from rectitude of which we find so many reports.

No one has done more to see that the services get their just rights and due need of credit than myself. If, therefore, I make a call upon them to do their part of national duty, I do so in full realisation of the fact that a large majority of them is actuated by patriotic motives and a spirit of service to the nation. They must, however, understand that the misdeeds of a few of them are as likely to injure the reputation of all as one dirty fish can proverbially spoil the whole tank. If the Legislature and Government place such large powers in their hands, they also place in them responsibility for using them properly. If they fail to discharge that responsibility, they not only render themselves unworthy of the service to which they belong but also show themselves underserving of the trust and confidence which the Government, the Legislature and the nation have reposed in them. Let them, therefore, so conduct themselves that every action of theirs brings as much good to the nation as possible without injuring anyone except the evildoer. If they can do so in this spirit, I am sure they will convert antipathy into sympathy, calumny into praise and sullenness into cooperation.

Finally, let me end on a personal note. Jawaharlal and I have been overwhelmed by the generous measure of confidence displayed in us. Having regard to the universality of that confidence, we naturally feel the terrible burden that we have to carry. That burden can be lightened only if we can secure all-round co-operation and support. My appeal to you all is, therefore, to extend to us and to the Government that cooperation and support and to help us in rooting out everything that retards the progress of the nation towards a better and happier state of things.

DISORDER HAMPERS PROGRESS

SPEECH AT
A PUBLIC MEETING,

CALCUTTA, 15 JANUARY 1950

I AM FULLY AWARE OF BENGAL'S AGONY. My heart goes out to the people of Bengal, but I am confident that, as always, they will face the difficulties with determination. Ever since India's freedom was at stake, Bengal has shown courage in every crisis. The leaders and the youth of Bengal endured great cruelties in the fight against alien rule. All India is indebted to Bengal for that. Later, when the alien grip was relaxed but the transition was still half-way through, the power was shared by the Muslim League and the British. That was a period of travail for you and you stood up to it courageously. Bengal or India can never forget what was the 'direct action' by those people. How can the plight of Calcutta in those days be forgotten? Nor can the subsequent event, in Noakhali forgotten by you or India. Those pages of history—good or bad, such as they are—cannot be deleted.

Gandhiji was there in those days. He walked from village to village and shared in the people's woes. He gave them sustenance and consolation. For a few days he stayed in Calcutta too. Then, either under provocation or in sympathy with you, our Bihari brethren showed their anger and the fire spread in India, particularly in the north. It came to be felt that unless the alien rule was removed somehow or the other, whatever their intentions, peace in the country was impossible, nor was it easy to remove the strife between the two communities. In the circumstances, we decided to accept partition of the country on the condition that Punjab and Bengal so be divided. It was God's will that when others wanted to partition Bengal, the people resisted the decision at great sacrifice, but partition of the same Bengal had to be accepted when there was no alternative dissenting voice was raised at that time because everyone understood that there was no other way out. We were clear in our minds that we could never accept Calcutta being taken away from us. The Muslim League leaders did not accept this. They were averse to having a 'moth-eaten' Pakistan. They wanted the whole of Bengal and the whole of Punjab. Ultimately they came round but the bloosdhed which then occurred has left a wound which will take some time to heal. Bengal's hurt is deep. Patience and endurance are needed, as on many previous occasions, but better days will come. We must do nothing to spoil things. We must act with discretion, not in anger.

In the part of Bengal that has separated from us, there are Hindus as well as Muslims. We want all of them to be happy. We want all wounds to heal a quickly. For this, patience and forbearance are needed on both sides.

Those who are our flesh and blood, those who fought by our side in the freedom struggle, cannot suddenly become foreign to us because they are on other side of a line. There are people in South Africa, people of Indian origin but with African citizenship, whom we still try to help. If they have a claim on us, surely those in that part of Bengal too have a claim. The bonds of kinship and economic and social links cannot be broken. But to remove their difficulties, we have first to set our own house in order.

Some people mislead the refugees who have come here and incite them by saying that the Government does nothing for them. But this does them no good. It does not mitigate their suffering. We can help them only if we set our house in order. We must stop the daily incidents of bomb and cracker blasts, burning of trains and cars, assaults on policemen, etc. Such occurrences distract attention from relief work. People elsewhere get the impression that lawlessness prevails

Vallabhbhai Patel

in Calcutta and living there is difficult. Only on coming there do they find that such is not the case. A handful of malcontent want to hold Calcutta and the Bengal Government in the grip of fear. I cannot understand their motives and intentions. I can understand a Communist ideology but how can such vandalism help? But what pains me more is the attitude of the lakhs of other residents of Calcutta. Why don't we understand our duty? It is wrong to think that combating lawlessness is the duty only of the police and the Government. Today's Government is not a foreign Government. A foreign Government would have used the old methods which we cannot use. Of course, when you feel you do not want this Government, you can remove it. We do not want to delay elections at all. A lot of money will have to be spent on the crores of people who have been enfranchised for the first time, but that does not matter. Much time and energy will have to be spent. Even that is of small consequence. What is needed even more is the right atmosphere. To those who think they have a substitute for the ballot box in the shape of revolution, I would respectfully submit that bombs and attacks on police are not revolution but a form of madness. It is the work of lunatics. I could understand if it were a few young men venting their frustrations in this way. But deliberate abetment of chaos helps no one. In the last war, a breakdown of the foreign Government's administration led to thirty lakh starvation deaths in Bengal. No one could protect them. But today when 70 per cent of the policemen are Bengalis themselves, what is the sense in attacking them? They impose restrictions for our own good, not on orders from any foreigners. Any threat to civil liberties comes not from them but from those who foster the terrorist cult. You have to stop them if you want to keep your liberty. You cannot pass the buck to the police. No democracy can be run with the policeman's baton. It has become a habit with us to blame the police. We have to change this attitude. It was another police whom we criticised night and day. Today they are our volunteers. We do not pay them as much as we ought to because we are unable to do so. But if you do not have sympathy for them in the work they are doing today, you will regret it.

I am aware of unemployment among the youth in Bengal. Thousands of young men in colleges are having difficulties with their studies because they have to work in shifts, something which used to happen only in factories. They have to work in these shifts and I can understand their difficulties and those of the professors. The forty or fifty thousand who graduate every year also face unemployment. Something has to be done about it. Calcutta is among India's biggest industrial centres. We need the kind of wealth produced in the city as much as we need the kind of wealth produced by farmers in the rural areas. Lack of one cannot be compensated by the other. But the Bengalis have the least share in this industrial sector. What is the reason for this? Those who own the factories and the companies have a duty towards the youth of Bengal. Similarly the unemployed youth of Bengal must understand that we cannot discriminate on the basis of provincialism. We have to discourage such narrow parochial influences.

Bengal has been left with a shrunken size after partition and there is a demand that some area from Bihar be added to it. I tried to do something about it but this is not easy because people have to be persuaded, the rulers and the people have to be persuaded, without precipitating any disorder. You must have seen how I brought round the 550–600 States without allowing any disorder to happen. Whoever indulged in disorder broke his head. You must help me in solving the Bengal problem similarly. Do not create trouble for me, do not put obstacles in my way. I want to do it; but for one thing I am beset by bodily troubles; for another, if I do not solve the other big problems in our country, they will affect you too and you will be in deeper trouble. That has to be avoided while your work is done. I want your cooperation so that we do not need so much police. I have never needed a policeman in my life, for who would want to kill me? But Gandhiji also said the same thing. So the police insists on following me around. We have to change this atmosphere by curbing the hot-heads amongst us. Similarly, our working people have to understand that they will be given their due; the owners and employers must give up their greed; the tradespeople must desist from black-marketeering and profiteering. Those who talk of China should remember that even Russia had to make immense sacrifices in its early years after the revolution. America, the world's wealthiest country, took seven years to frame its Constitution after independence. Ours is a vast country, yet we have framed our Constitution in three years in spite of all our troubles. America's wealth came from years of hard work. Much effort over many years went to make the present affluence. Our independence is only two years old and we want to have things shared out in portions. That would only make everyone poor and no one rich. I admit some of our people are rich but their riches are nothing compared to the riches of rich Americans. We want to use their wealth properly. Otherwise they will lose their wealth and we will gain nothing at all.

Inciting workers to strike, to go slow, to sit in, will damage us greatly. These things may be necessary sometimes, but not now. Our Indian traditions are such that we can sit down and arrive at agreements. The rich also have to be told their duty. They made a lot of black money under foreign rule during the war. They thought it was all right to avoid income-tax so that the alien rulers would get as little as possible. But now it helps neither them nor us. Some people want us to nationalise all industry. How are we to run nationalised industries if we cannot run our ordinary administration? It is easy to take over any industry we want to, but we do not have the resources to run them, enough experienced men, men of expertise and integrity. Today when we impose controls on business activities about which there are complaints, not one speaks well of those who administer the controls. We are burdened with complaints of bribery and Government gets a bad name. Gandhiji advised us to remove controls. So we made an experiment which landed us in so much trouble that there were demands for reimposition of controls. Now that we have imposed controls again, some people say Government does not know its own mind. They are right but much of the Government work in this vast country depended, for its disposal, on the prestige of the Englishmen who manned a little over a half of our administrative services and who have now departed. Today you see no English face among our policemen. British governors have left only their statues behind. What else is revolution if not this?

What we do in the next five years is going to shape India's future. All of you, the employees and the employers, the young and the old, men and women, have to work together to build up the country, eschewing strife, embracing the ways of peace and persuasion. If we spread poison and create provincial jealousies, the only result will be a flight of Calcutta's industries to places where there is greater peace. I would appeal to Bengal's youth, in this formative period when their character are being moulded, to control their minds, get ready to work in industry and learn to work the Government. You must not adopt the attitude that it is none of your business or concern. When a tram or a bus carrying fifty passengers is stopped by two young men and the passengers are asked to get down, they have no business to obey like a flock of sheep.

APPENDIX

THREE YEARS OF FREEDOM

INDEPENDENCE DAY MESSAGE,

NEW DELHI, 15 AUGUST 1950

TODAY WE ARE CELEBRATING THE THIRD ANNIVERSARY OF INDEPENDENCE. Looking back at the broad sweep of events since we became free, my predominant feeling is one of thankfulness and relief. We are grateful to Providence for having seen the country safely out of many a critical period. We have been able to survive many trials and difficulties which lay in our path.

In the world of today every country has to tread warily along the road to recovery from the legacies of the last war. We have had to be doubly cautious because, in addition to the troubles which a distracted world at large faces today, we had our own peculiar problems, problems which affected the very roots of our existence, tested every fibre of our being, reacted on the very fundamentals of our life and touched the very foundations of our infant democracy.

There are bound to be different reactions to our survival. Some will call it the miracle of our staying power. Some may say that the country has escaped a worse fate in spite of us. Many will probably give us the credit for having muddled through our difficulties.

We, as Government, of course, claim that despite our shortcomings the ship of State has been steered safely through the many rocks and shoals that lay in its course. Whatever the views, I am confident of one thing—namely, that if we have survived, it is because of our own intrinsic efforts, in whatever directions they may have been exerted. We have relied on ourselves, whether in the external or the internal domain, and it is that self-reliance which has enable us to achieve consolidation at home and prestige abroad.

Today, therefore, if I have faith in the future, it is based on this spirit of self-reliance. Nevertheless, I would not be true to myself if I did not confess to a sense of apprehension and anxiety. Certain tendencies and developments in our administrative and public affairs fill me with some disquiet and sadness of heart. The country can realise the feelings of one who has spent the major part of his public life in witnessing epics of sacrifice and selfless endeavour and feats of discipline and unity, and who now finds enacted before him scenes which mock at the past.

Our public life seems to be degenerating into a fen of stagnant waters; our conscience is troubled with doubts and despair about the possibilities of improvement. We do not seem to be profiting either from history or experience. We appear helplessly to be watching the sickle of time taking away the rich corn in us, leaving behind the bare and withered stalks.

Yet the tasks, that confront us are as complex and taxing as ever. They demand the best in us while we face them with indifferent resources. We seem to devote too much time to things that hardly matter and too little to those that count. We talk while the paramount need is that of action. We are critical of other people's exertions, but lack the will to contribute our own. We are trying to overtake others by giant strides while we have hardly learnt to walk.

On this, the third milestone of our career as a free country, I hope my countrymen will forgive me if I have tried to turn the searchlight inwards. In my life, I have now reached a stage when time is of the essence. Age has not diminished the passion which I hear to see my country great and to ensure that the foundations of our freedom are well and securely laid. Bodily infirmity has not dimmed my ardour to exert my utmost for the peace, prosperity and advancement of the

Motherland. But 'the bird of time has a little way to fly, and lo! it is on the wing'.

With all the sincerity and earnestness at my command and claiming the privilege of age, I, therefore, appeal to my fellow countrymen on this solemn and auspicious day to reflect on what they see in and around themselves and, with the strength and faith that comes from self-introspection, sustain the hope and confidence which an old servant of theirs still has in the future of our country.

Sources

'Speech at the First Meeting of the Advisory Committee on Fundamental Rights' from B. Shiva Rao, ed., *The Framing of the Indian Constitution*, Vol. I (Delhi: 1966).

'First Tidings First'; 'Forget Your Mutual Quarrels'; 'The Mantle Will Now Fall on Young Shoulders'; 'The Right Atmosphere'; 'Build a Strong India'; 'In Years to Come'; 'Blueprint for Prosperity'; 'Disorder Hampers Progress'; and 'Three Years of Freedom' from *For a United India: Speeches of Sardar Patel, 1947–1950* (New Delhi: Publications Division, Government of India, 1967).